WE TWO BROTHERS

Sharon Rogers

PAGE PUBLISHING
Conneaut Lake, PA

First originally published by Page Publishing 2024

ISBN 979-8-88960-406-8 (pbk)
ISBN 979-8-88960-407-5 (digital)

Printed in the United States of America

To Annie Ruth Brown, my mother who showed me how to be a great babysitter at the age of eight. To all the beautiful people in my life: Alfonso, Ed, James, Patrick, Kenneth, Fred, Marshall, Jermaine, Rico, Andre, Freddie, James Jr., Tevin, Jamall, Joel, Kavseon, Sonia, Tammy, Sherry, Donna, Kay, Linda, Vanessa, Rashell, Tara, Sherry, Tiffany, Sasha, Brittany, Shakayla, Rudy, Kiari, Da`Kyron, Sydney, Preston, JaMauri, Caiden, Roman, Freddie III, KD, Kamryn, Josiah, Erica, Harper, Jack and Jadairian, Jaleeha, Marlie, Nayeli, and Leonidas.

My mom says that before we were born, there were two eggs—one egg for my brother and one egg for me. We were born at a hospital in Union City, Tennessee.

My name is Patrick, and my brother's name is Kenneth. We do everything together.

When we look in the mirror, we see two identical faces looking back at us. He has my face, and I have his face. That's because we are twins.

We are best friends.
We play together.

We laugh together.
We read together.

We eat together. We join the choir together because we love to sing.

We do our chores together.

We go to school together.

At school, we play football, basketball, and soccer and run track together. We even have chicken pox together.

Where he goes, I go.
My mom says we are inseparable.

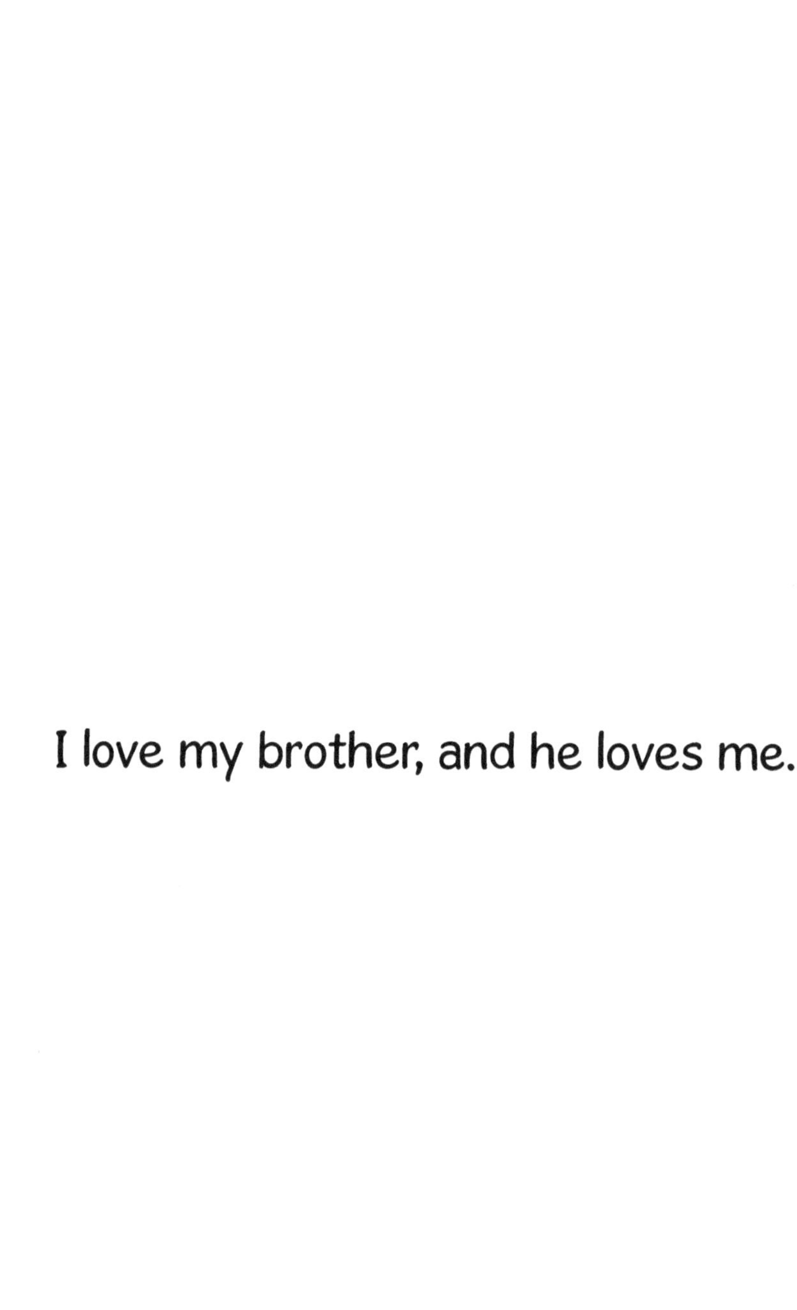

I love my brother, and he loves me.

We two plan to grow up together.

We are going to the army together because we are warriors, we are soldiers, we love to swim, we love boats, and we love driving trucks. And we will become sergeants together, and we always stand up for what is right.

We will get married and have our own boys.
We will grow old together.

We will always be best friends. We will tell our children and grandchildren about us growing up together.

We will sit on the front porch and remember
when it was just us two brothers.

About the Author

Sharon Rogers is a native of Hickman, Kentucky. She graduated with a bachelor's degree in home economics majoring in child development from Murray State University and also holds a master's degree in Education, Instructional Technology from American InterContinental University. She has been writing since high school. She creates stories from her family photo albums. She uses her past and present experiences to uplift young children and motivate them to be all they can be no matter their age. As a Head Start teacher, she would write stories about her students to make them laugh. She spends her free time doing motivational speaking for teenagers, braiding hair, writing children's short stories and poetry, and running the Mrs. Sharon Reading Corner for young children online (https://www.youtube.com/channel/UCvWfNA8jnjSHu-ToxR5Pr7w). She also enjoys shopping, and spending time with her family and Christian friends. She currently resides in Lansing, Michigan, with her wonderful husband, Alfonso.